BEING YOUR OWN STEWARD

A Practical Guide To Taking Charge Of Your Money

TORRIE SCOTT

AF721860

Copyright © 2026 by Torrie Scott

All rights reserved. This book or any portion thereof may not be reproduced or used in any manner whatsoever without the express written permission of the publisher except for the use of brief quotations in a book review.

Printed in the United States of America

First Edition, 2026

PAPERBACK ISBN: 979-8-2560-4561-6

EBOOK ISBN: 979-8-2560-4562-3

Red Pen Edits and Consulting

Info@redpeneditsllc.com

TABLE OF CONTENTS

DEDICATION

I dedicate this work to God: my Provider, my Teacher, and the One who has guided every step of my stewardship journey.

Your Word has been my foundation. You have shown me that wisdom begins with preparation (Luke 14:28), that blessing follows obedience (Deuteronomy 15:4–6), and that true freedom comes when I am no longer bound by debt (Proverbs 22:7; Proverbs 22:26–27).

You taught me to build my life in order, tending to what You have entrusted to me before reaching for more (Proverbs 24:27), to store wisely and not waste what You've provided (Proverbs 21:20), and to place my hope not in wealth, but in You alone, the Giver of all good things (1 Timothy 6:17–18).

Through generosity, You remind me that I am blessed to be a blessing (2 Corinthians 9:11). Through tithing, You invite me to honor You first and trust in Your promise to provide more than enough (Malachi 3:8–11; Matthew 23:23; Proverbs 3:9). And through it all, You call me to store up treasures in heaven, where my heart continually finds its home (Matthew 6:20–21).

Lord, thank You for teaching me stewardship, discipline, and generosity. May this book reflect Your wisdom, bring clarity to others, and honor You in every word.

INTRODUCTION

Money is not the goal. Money is a tool. A tool that works for you or against you, depending on how you manage it. This guidebook will help you understand your current financial situation, where you want to be, and how to bridge the gap using clear steps, simple systems, and practical exercises.

This isn't just about budgeting. It's about stewardship, taking responsibility, creating structure, and positioning yourself for peace, freedom, and generosity.

This guide and workbook will help you:

- Build control and confidence
- Eliminate confusion and overwhelm
- Create a realistic plan
- Pay off debt
- Build savings

empty bank account. You begin planning ahead. You create space for savings, build buffers for emergencies, and gain the ability to enjoy your money without guilt or confusion.

Ultimately, being aware of how you spend money is about more than numbers on a page. It's about taking ownership of your financial life, breaking unhelpful cycles, and creating a clear path toward stability, freedom, and peace. When you understand your spending, you're no longer just surviving. You're stewarding your resources with purpose and confidence.

Your journey from Point A to Point B begins with the **Five Be's of Financial Stewardship**.

CHAPTER 2

THE FIVE BE'S OF FINANCIAL STEWARDSHIP

Understanding You're Spending Through 30-Day Bank Statements & the Five Be's

Reviewing your bank statements from the past thirty days (if your first time, do 90 days to establish a pattern of habits) is one of the most effective ways to discover how you truly spend your money. This simple step provides a clear, honest picture of your financial habits, showing where your money is going, where it's being wasted, and what areas need more structure. By identifying unnecessary purchases, impulse spending, forgotten subscriptions, or unplanned expenses, you gain the clarity needed to make intentional financial decisions.

What to Do

- Start using a **Zero-Based Budget**
- Choose your budgeting style: monthly, bi-weekly, or weekly
- Create a **Stability Fund** with a $1,000 goal

WORKBOOK EXERCISE: Your Stability Fund Plan

1. My monthly income:

   ____

2. My first savings goal: $1,000
3. Amount I can save weekly/bi-weekly:

   ____

4. Estimated date to reach $1,000:

   ____

2. Be Free

Why Living Debt-Free Matters

Living debt-free is one of the most powerful steps toward financial stability and peace. When we speak of being debt-free, we are specifically referring to freeing yourself from credit card debt, one of the most common and expensive forms of debt. Credit cards often carry high interest rates that keep people stuck in a cycle of monthly payments, rising balances, and ongoing financial stress.

Removing this burden protects your income, reduces pressure, and allows you to take control of your financial future. While it *is* okay to have a credit card, it should be used only when there is absolutely no other option, true emergencies, life-or-death situations, or moments where immediate access is essential for your safety or survival. It should never be used for day-to-day spending.

By eliminating unnecessary credit card use and living without consumer debt, you gain freedom to save, invest, and build a healthier financial foundation. You strengthen your confidence, reduce stress, and put yourself in a position to make intentional decisions that reflect your values and long-term goals. Living debt-free is not about restriction. It's about creating stability, clarity, and lasting peace in your financial life.

Simply stated: Freedom comes from eliminating the weight of debt.

What to Do

- Use the **Debt Snowball Method (discussed in chapter 6)**

WORKBOOK EXERCISE: List Your Debts Smallest to Largest

Debt Name	Balance	Minimum

3. Be Prepared

Why It's Important to Build a Security Savings Fund (3–6 Months of Expenses)

A Security Savings Fund, often called an emergency fund, is one of the most powerful tools in financial stewardship. It serves as your personal safety net, ensuring that you can handle unexpected events without falling into crisis or slipping back into debt. Life is unpredictable. Jobs change, medical needs arise, cars break down, and unexpected expenses show up at the worst times. Without a financial buffer, even a small emergency can create significant stress and derail your progress.

Building a savings fund with 3 to 6 months of living expenses creates stability and

WORKBOOK EXERCISE: Monthly Living Expenses

Total monthly expenses: ________________

3 months saved equals: _________________

6 months saved equals: _________________

4. Be Generous

Why Being Generous Matters

Being generous is an essential part of financial stewardship because it shifts your mindset from scarcity to abundance. Generosity helps you stay grounded, grateful, and aware of the blessings you already have. When you give to others, whether through your time, resources, or financial support, you create a healthier relationship with money. Instead of holding onto it out of fear, you learn to use it with purpose. Generosity not only strengthens communities and supports those in need, it also builds character, humility, and joy within your own life. Giving makes you more intentional, more compassionate, and more connected to the values that truly matter. In short, generosity enriches both the giver and the receiver, making it a powerful part of living a balanced, meaningful, and financially healthy life.

Simply stated: Generosity resets your mindset from survival to stewardship.

What to Do

- Give 10% (tithe)
- Pay yourself (savings)
- Support others when possible

REFLECTION EXERCISE

How does generosity fit into your life?

5. Be Blessed

How to Be Blessed

Being blessed is the stage where peace, stability, and abundance come together as a result of wise financial stewardship. It's not just about having more money. It's about living with confidence, purpose, and balance. When you follow the principles of budgeting, saving, giving, and responsible decision-making, you create a life that feels steady and secure. This stability frees you from constant financial stress and gives you room to grow, plan, and enjoy what you've worked hard for. Abundance flows naturally when you manage your resources well, make intentional choices, and stay focused on long-term goals. To be blessed is to live in a place where your finances support your life, not control it, allowing you to experience greater peace, gratitude, and fulfillment.

Simply stated: This is where peace, stability, and abundance come together.

What to Do

- Build wealth intentionally
- Maintain the habits you've developed
- Continue becoming a responsible steward of what you have

CHAPTER 3

PRIMARY LIVING COST (PLC): PROTECTING YOUR ESSENTIALS

Why It's Important to Pay These Four Essentials First

Prioritizing **Food, Utilities, Shelter, and Transportation** ensures that your basic needs are protected before anything else. These four essentials keep your household stable, safe, and functioning. By covering them first, you prevent immediate crises such as hunger, loss of electricity or water, eviction, or being unable to get to work. When these core needs are met, you can approach the rest of your finances with clarity and confidence. Paying these essentials first creates a strong foundation, reduces stress, and allows you to make better financial decisions. No matter what your income level or financial situation looks like, securing these priorities is the first step toward stability, stewardship, and long-term financial health.

Simply stated: Before you pay anything else, these four categories come first.

1. **Food**
2. **Utilities (electricity, water, sewage)**
3. **Shelter (rent or mortgage)**
4. **Transportation (car payment and car insurance payment)**

These ensure your household is secure while you work on budgeting and debt.

WORKBOOK EXERCISE: PLC Breakdown

Food: ________________

Utilities: ________________

Housing: ________________

Transportation: ________________

Total: ________________

This number helps you understand how much it costs to keep your household stable.

CHAPTER 4
HOW TO GET OUT OF DEBT

Debt-Free Living Begins With Simple Habits

Debt-free living doesn't start with big, overwhelming changes. It begins with small, consistent habits that shift the way you manage your money. Simple actions like tracking your spending, creating a budget, avoiding unnecessary purchases, and paying just a little extra toward your smallest debt can create powerful momentum. These habits help you stay aware, stay disciplined, and stay motivated as you move toward financial freedom. Over time, the small steps add up, turning intentional choices into long-term success. When you master the basics, you build a strong

CHAPTER 5
ZERO-BASED BUDGETING

Why Zero-Based Budgeting Is Important

Zero-based budgeting is important because it gives every dollar a clear purpose, helping you take full control of your finances. Instead of wondering where your money went, this system tells your money exactly where to go. By assigning each dollar to a category, whether it's bills, savings, debt, or everyday spending, you eliminate waste, increase awareness, and make intentional financial decisions. Zero-based budgeting ensures that your income and expenses balance to zero, bringing structure, clarity, and discipline to your financial life. This method not only prevents overspending but also helps you prioritize your goals, build savings, and stay on track with long-term financial stability. In short, zero-based budgeting is a simple but powerful tool for creating order, confidence, and financial peace.

Simply stated, A Zero-Based Budget means:

Income – Expenses = 0

Every dollar has a purpose and a job, even if that job is savings.

Steps for Creating Your Zero-Based Budget

1. Write down your income
2. List all expenses (anything you spend your money on but remember to start with your PLC
3. Assign every dollar to a category
4. Track your spending each week (Get a notebook and keep it simple)
5. Adjust as needed

Note additional expenses can be cable, internet, car maintenance, alarm system, apps, gas, nails, hair, outing with friends, pet food, pet vet visits, clothes, etc.

WORKBOOK EXERCISE: Your Zero-Based Budget

Category	Amount Budgeted	Amount Spent	Difference
Income			
Food			
Utilities			
Housing			
Gas / Transport			
Debt Payments			
Saving			
Other			

CHAPTER 6
THE DEBT SNOWBALL APPROACH (HOW IT WORKS)

How the Snowball Approach Works

The Snowball Approach is a simple and highly motivating method for paying off debt. You begin by listing all your debts from smallest to largest, regardless of interest rate. Then, you attack the smallest debt first while continuing to pay the minimum balance on all your other debts. Once the smallest debt is paid off, you roll the payment you were using for that debt onto the next one, creating a "snowball" effect. As you repeat this process, your payments increase in size and your progress becomes more rapid. This momentum builds confidence and keeps you motivated, helping you eliminate all your debt step by step until you are completely debt-free.

Steps:

1. List all debts from smallest to largest
2. Attack the smallest debt first
3. Pay minimums on all other debts
4. Once one debt is paid off, roll that payment to the next
5. Repeat until all debt is eliminated

This method builds momentum and confidence. Your financial snowball grows as you go.

WORKBOOK EXERCISE: The Snowball Tracker

Debt	Balance	Min. Payment	Snowball Payment	Estimated Payoff Date

CHAPTER 7

BUILDING WEALTH: WHAT HAPPENS AFTER DEBT

Once your debt is eliminated and your savings are established, you can move into the next level of stewardship: building wealth intentionally.

Wealth-building isn't about being rich — it's about having *options, stability, and generational impact.* Wealth creates space for choice.

The Core Wealth-Building Steps

1. Eliminate debt (you are already working on this)
2. Build a fully funded Security Savings fund

My First Wealth-Building Goal

I will begin by focusing on:

____

By this date: ________________________

CHAPTER 8
LONG-TERM STEWARDSHIP HABITS

Wealth isn't just built. It is **maintained** through habits.

Here are the habits of excellent stewards:

1. Monthly Budget Meetings

Set a recurring "money meeting" with yourself (or your partner) every month.

Agenda:

- Review last month
- Adjust next month
- Prepare for upcoming expenses
- Celebrate progress

2. Track & Audit Regularly

Your financial health depends on awareness.

- Track spending weekly
- Review bank statements monthly
- Audit expenses quarterly

3. Live Below Your Means

This creates margin, the space where savings and generosity grow.

4. Keep the PLC's First

Never let budgeting stress take away essentials:

- Food
- Utilities
- Shelter
- Transportation

5. Continue Learning

Stewardship grows when your knowledge grows:

- Books
- Workshops
- Financial coaching (for more information, go to the footnotes)
- Online courses

WORKBOOK EXERCISE: My Monthly Stewardship Routine

Choose your rhythm:

- Weekly check-in day: ________________________
- Monthly budget meeting date: _____________
- Quarterly review months: ____________________

adjustment is part of the process, and every step forward counts.

This plan helps you stay on track from month to month.

Below is a simple year-long structure.

MONTHS 1–3

Focus: Stability & Awareness

- Build $1,000 Stability Fund
- Begin Zero-Based Budgeting
- List all debts, smallest to largest
- Reduce unnecessary spending

Journal Prompt:

"What financial habits am I building during these first 90 days?"

MONTHS 4–6

Focus: Debt Momentum

- Begin Debt Snowball
- Sell unused items
- Explore part-time income opportunities
- Maintain your Four Walls

Journal Prompt:

"What progress have I made so far?"

____

____

MONTHS 7–9

Focus: Preparation

- Continue the debt snowball
- Explore beginner investing courses
- Identify long-term goals (house payoff, retirement)

Journal Prompt:

"What future goals motivate me most?"

MONTHS 10–12

Focus: Growth

- Finish remaining debts or reduce them significantly
- Increase savings
- Plan next year's financial goals

Journal Prompt:

"What does the next level of stewardship look like for me?"

CHAPTER 10
YOUR STEWARDSHIP TOOLBOX

This chapter summarizes the tools you will use throughout the journey.

1. The Zero-Based Budget

Gives every dollar a job.

2. The Primary Living Cost (PLC)

Protects your stability.

3. The Debt Snowball

Gives you speed and momentum.

4. The Stability Fund ($1,000)

Provides immediate protection.

5. The Security Savings Fund (3–6 months)

Prepares you for emergencies.

6. Monthly Money Meetings

Maintains structure.

7. Learning & Coaching

Expands your understanding.

8. Generosity & Giving

Keeps your heart in stewardship mode.

Why Opening the Right Bank Accounts Matters

Opening a bank account with both a checking and savings account is an essential first step in building a strong financial foundation. A checking account helps you manage everyday transactions, while a savings account separates the money you're setting aside for future needs, goals, or emergencies. Choosing a reputable credit union can be especially helpful because they often offer lower fees, better customer service, and more favorable loan rates than traditional banks. Additionally, placing your savings in a high-yield savings account allows your money to grow faster through higher interest rates, helping you build your emergency fund and long-term savings more efficiently. By using the right combination of accounts, checking for daily expenses, credit unions for member-focused benefits, and high-yield savings for growth, you set yourself up for better money management, stronger financial protection, and long-term financial success.

WORKBOOK EXERCISE: My Top Three Tools

Which tools will you focus on first?

1. ______________________________
2. ______________________________
3. ______________________________

CHAPTER 11

COMMON ROADBLOCKS (AND HOW TO OVERCOME THEM)

Even with a great plan, challenges happen.

Here's how to stay on track.

Roadblock 1: Overspending

Solution: Track weekly and create spending categories.

Roadblock 2: Unexpected Expenses

Solution: Use your Stability Fund or Security Savings Fund.

Roadblock 3: Income is too tight

Solution: Temporary part-time job, selling unused items or create a passive income business.

Roadblock 4: Discouragement

Solution: Celebrate progress, no matter how small.

Roadblock 5: Lack of accountability

Solution: Use a coach, mentor, or trusted friend.

WORKBOOK EXERCISE: My Current Roadblocks

What challenges are you facing?

What solutions can you apply?

CHAPTER 12
COMMITMENT TO STEWARDSHIP

Before financial change becomes visible on the outside, it starts with a decision on the inside.

This is your commitment to:

- Take charge
- Stay consistent
- Practice discipline
- Maintain generosity
- Become the steward you were meant to be

MY COMMITMENT STATEMENT

"I commit to being a faithful steward of my resources. I will take responsibility, stay consistent, and use my money wisely so I can build stability, freedom, and abundance for myself and my family."

WRITE YOUR OWN COMMITMENT STATEMENT

____

____

____

____

____

Signature: ______________________

Date: ___________________________

ABOUT THE AUTHOR

TORRIE SCOTT

Torrie Scott was born in Washington, D.C. and raised as a proud military brat alongside her three brothers. The daughter of George and Linda Scott, she grew up in a family rooted in discipline, resilience, and service. A gifted athlete, Torrie earned a basketball scholarship and began her academic journey at Northeast

Community College, where she completed her Associate of Liberal Arts degree. She later continued her education at Furman University, graduating with a Bachelor of Science in Health and Exercise, and later obtained her Master of Business Administration from Strayer University.

With more than 20 years of leadership experience in the telecommunications industry, Torrie built a strong professional foundation, until being laid off in 2023 prompted a major shift in her life's direction. Instead of viewing the moment as a setback, she embraced it as an opportunity to pursue her passion: helping others achieve financial clarity, stability, and confidence.

Torrie's financial expertise is not just academic. It is personal. Through years of trial, error, and hard-earned lessons, she learned how money truly works. After experiencing financial strain caused by a lack of knowledge and unwise decisions in her early years, she became committed to breaking unhealthy cycles. By applying the same principles found in this book, Torrie successfully eliminated debt multiple times, rebuilt her financial foundation, and transformed her relationship with money.

Her mission now is to share what she has learned, to equip youth, young adults, and individuals of all ages with the tools, wisdom, and practical steps needed to manage money with purpose. Torrie believes financial stewardship is more than numbers; it is a pathway to freedom, stability, and peace. Through this guidebook, she hopes to empower others to take charge of their finances and build a stronger future for themselves and their families.

"Steward Your Money. Strengthen Your Future."

THANK YOU TO MY READERS

Thank you for choosing this book and allowing me to be part of your financial journey. Your decision to invest in your growth, your stability, and your future is powerful, and I am truly grateful you trusted these pages to guide you. I hope that the tools, principles, and encouragement inside this book bring clarity and confidence to your financial life.

If you would like more personalized support, I also provide financial coaching and would be honored to walk with you as you build a healthier relationship with money. You can reach me directly at **torriescottwfg@gmail.com**.

Thank you again for your support, and please consider purchasing this book as a gift for someone who could benefit from financial clarity, practical tools, and a fresh start. Together, we can help more people experience stability, freedom, and peace.

www.ingramcontent.com/pod-product-compliance
Lightning Source LLC
LaVergne TN
LVHW050923210926
848482LV00012B/515
* 9 7 9 8 2 5 6 0 4 5 6 1 6 *